A *DISCIPLESHIP JOURNAL* BIBLE • STUDY ON
OVERCOMING OVERLOAD

BEATING
BUSYNESS

BY ADAM R. HOLZ

NAVPRESS ◑
BRINGING TRUTH TO LIFE
P.O. Box 35001, Colorado Springs, Colorado 80935

OUR GUARANTEE TO YOU

We believe so strongly in the message of our books that we are making this quality guarantee to you. If for any reason you are disappointed with the content of this book, return the title page to us with your name and address and we will refund to you the list price of the book. To help us serve you better, please briefly describe why you were disappointed. Mail your refund request to: NavPress, P.O. Box 35002, Colorado Springs, CO 80935.

The Navigators is an international Christian organization. Our mission is to reach, disciple, and equip people to know Christ and to make Him known through successive generations. We envision multitudes of diverse people in the United States and every other nation who have a passionate love for Christ, live a lifestyle of sharing Christ's love, and multiply spiritual laborers among those without Christ.

NavPress is the publishing ministry of The Navigators. NavPress publications help believers learn biblical truth and apply what they learn to their lives and ministries. Our mission is to stimulate spiritual formation among our readers.

Visit the NavPress web site at: http://www.navpress.com/

ISBN 1-57683-155-8

Cover art by Stephanie Garcia

Excerpts from *His Gentle Voice*, ©1988, by Judith Couchman, are reprinted by permission of Multnomah Publishers, Inc.

Unless otherwise identified, all Scripture quotations in this publication are taken from the HOLY BIBLE: NEW INTERNATIONAL VERSION ® (NIV®), copyright © 1973, 1978, 1984 by International Bible Society. Used by permission of Zondervan Publishing House. All rights reserved. Other versions used include: *The Message: New Testament with Psalms and Proverbs* (MSG) by Eugene H. Peterson, copyright © 1993, 1994, 1995, used by permission of NavPress Publishing Group; the *Revised Standard Version Bible* (RSV), copyright © 1946, 1952, 1971 by the Division of Christian Education of the National Council of the Churches of Christ in the USA, used by permission, all rights reserved; the *New Testament in Modern English* (PH), J. B. Phillips translator, copyright© J. B. Phillips 1958, 1960, 1972, used by permission of Macmillan Publishing Company; *The Living Bible* (TLB), copyright © 1971, used by permission of Tyndale House Publishers, Inc., Wheaton, IL 60189, all rights reserved; the *Good News Bible: Today's English Version* (TEV), copyright © American Bible Society 1966, 1971, 1976; *The New English Bible* (NEB), copyright © 1961, 1970, The Delegates of the Oxford University Press and The Syndics of the Cambridge University Press; the *Contemporary English Version* (CEV), copyright © 1995 The American Bible Society, published under license from Thomas Nelson Publishers; the *Jerusalem Bible* (JB), copyright © 1966, 1967, and 1968 by Darton, Longman & Todd Ltd. and Doubleday & Company, Inc.; and the *King James Version* (KJV), the *New American Standard Bible* (NASB); © The Lockman Foundation 1960, 1962, 1963, 1968, 1971, 1972, 1973, 1975, 1977; Scripture quotations marked (NLT) are taken from the *Holy Bible, New Living Translation*, copyright © 1996. Used by permission of Tyndale House Publishers, Inc., Wheaton, Illinois 60189. All rights reserved.

Printed in the United States of America

1 2 3 4 5 6 7 8 9 10 / 05 04 03 02 01 00 99

FOR A FREE CATALOG OF
NAVPRESS BOOKS & BIBLE STUDIES,
CALL 1-800-366-7788 (USA)
OR 1-416-499-4615 (CANADA)

Contents

Introduction

The Plague of Busyness

Busyness, it seems, has become an endemic problem for many in our culture. Despite technological advances that have increased productivity and enhanced our communication, our to-do lists are as long as ever. Too many believers still feel ruled by what Charles Hummel called "the tyranny of the urgent."

In fact, with the number of ministry opportunities available to believers, we may be even more susceptible to the plague of busyness. How can we begin to deal with the frenetic pace of our lives?

Over the years, *Discipleship Journal* has published a number of articles addressing busyness. This study compiles some of those articles and combines them with discussion questions and innovative learning activities.

To enable you to tackle this issue head on in your life, this study will address some meaningful questions related to busyness, including the following:

- What does my life really look like?
- Why am I so busy?
- How do I set priorities biblically?
- How can I learn to discern God's will and hear His voice as I make decisions?
- What is my real mission in life?
- What roles should silence and personal retreat play in my life?

How This Study Guide Works

This *Discipleship Journal* Bible study may look a little different from study guides you have used in the past. In addition to the Scripture that you'll be looking at in each article, we've combed through issues of *Discipleship Journal* magazine and selected some of the best articles on a variety of topics essential to living life as a disciple of Christ in today's world.

This combination of Scripture texts and the sharpened insights of experienced communicators should give you plenty to contemplate as you discover what it means to follow Jesus in your life situation.

We have also put more emphasis on thinking about, praying over, meditating on, and wrestling with the meaning of a few key Scripture passages rather than quickly looking at as many verses as possible. You'll sometimes find multiple questions about a single passage that are intended to help you understand what the passage says, and how it applies to you personally. The idea is to help you to be a "doer" of the Word and not merely a "hearer" (James 1:22, RSV).

Not all questions incorporate specific verses of Scripture, but they all are intended to help you think through what it means to apply biblical truth. Sometimes that will involve changing the way you *think*, and often it will mean changing the way you *act*.

This study guide is designed to be used either individually or in a small group setting. (Your experience will likely be enhanced by the input, perspective, and prayers of other like-minded believers.) Even if you work on this study on your own, we encourage you to share your insights and discoveries with someone who can help "sharpen" you in your walk with God (see Proverbs 27:17).

Our prayer is that God's Word will both challenge and encourage you as you seek to follow Him "with all your heart and with all your soul and with all your mind and with all your strength" (Mark 12:30).

An Easy Yoke?

I rub my eyes and stare down at the legal pad in front of me. What stares back at me is my to-do list. It's not a pretty sight. It's covered with ten or twelve hurriedly drawn boxes, each of which is filled and spilling over with dozens of little scribbles: A phone call to return. A meeting to set up. A note to write. A sermon to prepare. A car to service. I feel overwhelmed.

Been there?

Don't you get the sense that something might be a bit out of kilter for us, driven as we are by our calendars and to-do lists? How do we face the daunting task of fitting together a busy life and career with God's kingdom purposes?

In this article, entitled **"Take a Load Off" by David Henderson** (excerpted from Issue 97), the author explores how we can find rest in the midst of the hectic lives many of us live. As you read each section, underline any portions that especially stand out to you. Then move on to the questions and exercises that follow.

 TAKE A LOAD OFF

Jesus said, "Come to me, all you who are weary and burdened, and I will give you rest. Take my yoke upon you and learn from me, for I am gentle and humble in heart, and you will find rest for your souls. For my yoke is easy and my burden is light" (Matthew 11:28-30).

We know the words well and find some comfort in them. But is this what we experience? An easy yoke? A light burden? Yokes and burdens, yes. But easy and light ones? Rest for the soul? No. Most of us strain against yokes that are very different, and far heavier, than Jesus intended for us.

So how do we shed our heavy loads and take on some lighter fare? Not easily. Still, it can be done. Notice something when you look back at that verse: two words — yoke and rest — are repeated twice in these three short sentences.

Rest is a word that suggests the stopping of motion — like turning off a car at the end of an eight-hour drive. The spark plugs cease firing, the pistons stop clamoring, and the engine comes to sudden stillness: resting, stopping, ceasing.

But notice that the rest Jesus promises is soul rest, not body rest. His concern is internal, at the level of the heart. He says that He will bring an end to the clamoring in our souls, introducing quiet and contentment in its place. So the image of rest that comes to mind of lounging in the sun on a Maui beach is probably not as accurate as, say, the picture of arriving at your car after you've just finished climbing one of Colorado's fourteen-thousand-foot peaks. Your body is spent, your feet are throbbing, but your soul is refreshed, alive, and quieted. The rest, the peace, is on the inside.

---

1. What is the main reason you're interested in a study focusing on busyness?

2. How do you feel about your level of busyness at the moment?

    ☐ It's manageable.
    ☐ I'm doing as much as I'm able to do.
    ☐ I'm feeling overwhelmed and exhausted.
    ☐ I'm frantic. If something doesn't change soon, I'll be on my way to breakdown!
    ☐ Other:

3. None of us can effectively begin to deal with the issue of busyness until we have a clear picture of what our lives look like. In the space below, write down each of the main activities on your schedule in a typical week, and the number of hours you spend on each. (Include things like work, fitness, sleep, reading, time with family or friends, and so on.)

4. a. The author focuses on a promise that at first seems paradoxical. Read Matthew 11:28-30 again.

   b. How would you describe your initial gut reaction to this promise? (For example: *Thank goodness Jesus understands that I'm weary and burdened*; or *Jesus says rest is possible, but I just don't see how.*)

5. Review the passage again and write in the space below the words that grab your attention. Then describe why you think you gravitate toward these words.

6. Jesus gives three specific commands in this passage: "Come to me . . . Take my yoke . . . learn from me." In your own life, what would you need to do to obey these commands? (For example: *I haven't been spending time regularly in God's Word. For me to come to Jesus, I need to spend time understanding what He wants for my life by reading the Bible.*)

7. a. Read how *The Message* translates Matthew 11:28-30:

   "Are you tired? Worn out? Burned out on religion? Come to me. Get away with me and you'll recover your life. I'll show you how to take a real rest. Walk with me and work with me— watch how I do it. Learn the unforced rhythms of grace. I won't lay anything heavy or ill-fitting on you. Keep company with me and you'll learn to live freely and lightly."

   b. The phrase "unforced rhythms of grace" is used in this passage to describe the kind of life Jesus promises. With this in mind, are there certain areas of your life that feel forced right now? If so, what are they?

D The word yoke is also an interesting one. I suspect we all know that the word describes one of those big, clunky, wooden contraptions that goes over the shoulders of an ox and attaches to a plow that follows behind. In Jesus' day, the word yoke was also a synonym for obligations, the sum of all the duties that someone had to shoulder to fulfill a commitment in a certain area.

So rest and yoke are nearly opposites. The unexpected twist was that Jesus brought these two words together to describe what happens when we follow Him. When we take on His yoke, He said, we experience the unexpected: rest.

Rephrasing Jesus' words, then, we come up with something like this: "Come to Me, all you who are worn out and weighed down by scrambling to meet the demands of others, and I will bring quiet to your spirits. Serve Me, follow Me, and—because I am caring and understanding—I will stop the clamoring in your souls. For what I ask of you is not a burden at all."

8. a. In the space below, make a quick sketch of an ox cart or wagon. Then go back to the list of commitments you identified in question three, page 9. For each item on your schedule, draw a box on the ox cart. Make the boxes large or small in proportion to the amount of time and emotional energy they require.

b. Assuming that the yoke attached to this cart rests on your shoulders, how has "loading the cart" by drawing a picture of your obligations changed the way you see the weight of your yoke?

☐ My yoke is not as heavy as I'd thought.
☐ My yoke is about as heavy as I'd assumed.
☐ My yoke is much more burdensome than I'd realized.

9. Jesus doesn't promise to get rid of our yoke altogether. Rather
    He says He will replace it with a yoke that is easy, or appro-
    priate to our capacity. How do you think an easy yoke would
    look different from the yoke you're wearing now?

D Busy, Busy, Busy

Look what happens to most of us when we come into the kingdom.
We enter the kingdom on the sole basis of our having received
what God handed to us. But what happens once we're in? We
throw ourselves into serving this King of ours, and our schedules
begin to get stuffed with important things to do.

Now, let me be clear that there is nothing inherently wrong
with hard work or a full schedule. But how and why we busy ourselves is a different story. I think our frantic busyness belies our real
convictions about service and ministry. We act as if it is all up to us.
As though something were at stake. As though it would not get
done if we didn't do it. As though our significance were somehow
tied up in it. As though our well-being and God's pleasure—in fact
our whole relationship with God—depended upon it.

But it is not all up to us. When we apply Matthew 11:28-30 to
our busy lives and schedules, we need to come to grips with this:
not only faith but the whole of life and ministry must be understood simply as a response to the initiative of a gracious God. He
will lead us into the work and ministry He has for us, and we simply get the adventure of holding on tight to His hand and enjoying
the ride.

Ephesians 2:10 tells us, "For we are God's workmanship, created in Christ Jesus to do good works, which God prepared in
advance for us to do."

That means instead of cramming our lives full of things calcu-
lated to please God, we can be led into acts of ministry that God
has already planned ahead for us, confident of the pleasure God
takes in us through Christ. He will lead us into it, He will show us

how to do it, He will provide everything we need to complete it, and He will bring about His desired results through it.

But how do I do that? Let me suggest several steps that might prove helpful as you begin to discover God's lighter load for you.

10. a. Ephesians 2:10 sheds further light on God's intentions for our work and ministry. Spend a few moments thinking about the following three phrases from that verse, then rewrite each one in your own words.

- "For we are God's workmanship, . . ."

- "created in Christ Jesus to do good works, . . ."

- "which God prepared in advance for us to do."

b. How do these truths encourage or challenge you in your current situation? (For example: *Because God made me, He knows better than I do what my capacity is for ministry activities. I need to spend more time in prayer before saying yes to commitments.*)

D Strip Off Your Self-Made Yokes

We need to recognize and lay aside the many things we busy ourselves with that God has not called us to do. Every week there seems to show up on my schedule—and maybe on yours as well—at least one thing I have taken on simply because it gets me something.

How do we recognize the yokes of our own making? Over the years I've discovered some simple questions that can help me begin to recognize those impostors:

13

- What is the real motivation for what I am doing? Am I doing this to meet some need in myself? To prove something? To gain something? To avoid something?
- Who am I trying to please—myself? Others? God?
- Why do I feel compelled to do this? Do I feel as though something is at stake? What would happen if I waited or didn't do it at all?

11. Go back to your list of regular commitments from question three, page 9. Choose one thing on your schedule that adds stress to your life and consider it in light of the previous three questions. What conclusions did you reach.

Ⓓ Make Yourself Open and Available

Seeking God's kingdom needs to be the highest desire in our lives. Glorifying God, seeking and saving the lost, laying down my life for my brothers and sisters, obeying divine intentions—are those really the things that give shape to my life? Have I really made the things that matter most to God the things that matter most to me?

Jeremiah expressed this attitude in a beautiful way when he wrote, "I know, O Lord, that a man's life is not his own; it is not for man to direct his steps" (Jeremiah 10:23). We are not our own, but His. And His desire is that we would be wholly so.

Therefore, we must come before God on a daily basis and give the whole of our lives to Him. We must lift the specifics of today and our future days before the Lord. We can ask Him to sift through those many options that vie for our time and attention and to show us the handful that are part of His timeless intention for that day. As I've come to understand it, that means making ourselves open for whatever God wants to do in us and making ourselves available for whatever it is that God desires to do through us. Open and available—that is the type of person God uses.

12. Read Mark 1:21. What does this verse reveal about how Jesus made Himself available to God?

13. How does prayer make us open and available to God?

D Build In Pockets of Time for Reflection

The emptiest lives are those stuffed with motion from morning to night. It is only when we have elbow room built into our days and into our lives that we become still enough for God to speak to us.

It is not a coincidence that the phrases "wait on the Lord" and "be still" are found so often in the Scriptures. Regular time to quiet your spirit before God and ask what God seems to be saying, how He seems to be moving, and where He seems to be leading is crucial. Intentional prayer about the demands of the day, moments of quiet between appointments, and monthly retreats to break from your normal routine—all of these are pauses that put us within reach of God's voice. We should see them as nonnegotiable ways of wetting our finger and holding it up in the air to see which way the wind of God's Spirit is moving around us. How else will we be able to discern which activities are a waste of time and to identify areas not yet considered that should be at the top of our list?

14. According to the author, what are some of the purposes of being still and waiting on the Lord?

15. Read Isaiah 40:28-31. What are some of the benefits of waiting on the Lord found in these verses?

16. How does busyness make it difficult to wait on the Lord?

17. Which passage of Scripture in this lesson touched you most deeply? Write this passage on a sticky note and put it where you'll notice it. Reflect on it throughout the week.

18. *Optional Exercise*: To further help you understand how you use your time, keep a time log for the next week. Write down all of the ways you spend your time throughout the week. Like money, time tends to slip away. A time log may help you see more clearly how you use your time.

Words Worth Remembering

The question to ask at the end of life's race is not so much "What have I accomplished?" but "Whom have I loved, and how courageously?"

—Geoff Gorsuch, from "Journey to Adelphos," Issue 14

2

Why Am I So Busy?

The following article, entitled "**Just Say No**" **by Howard R. Macy** (excerpted from Issue 60), examines what motivates us to accept certain commitments and why it is sometimes difficult to say no. As you read the article, underline the thoughts that stand out to you, then move on to the questions and exercises that follow.

D JUST SAY NO

Karen rushed up to me after the benediction and poured out her frustration over how frantic she was with all she had to do. "Last week I almost had a breakdown," she said. "What am I going to do?"

It was a good question. Karen is a bright, ambitious young woman who can't say no to anything worthwhile. The old adage "If you want something done, ask a busy person to do it" fits her perfectly. She can do almost anything well, except say no. What, indeed, was she going to do?

Karen knew, of course, that she was asking an expert, for I'm a person who excels in making bad choices. I have often been in precisely her predicament. But I've also begun to understand why, even though I still make mistakes. One thing I've learned is that the pressure comes from me more than from others. By and large, nobody makes me take on the overload of commitments that destroy any reasonable schedule and drain my energy.

I've also learned that the cure for my problem is more spiritual than mechanical. No doubt overcommitted people find help in better time management techniques, as I have, but many of them will use their newfound skills to pack more obligation into their lives rather than to step back from the madcap pace. As they get better, they also get worse, mostly because they are ignoring the causes while dealing with the symptoms. The real solution is to learn the reasons why we say yes when we should say no. Most of those are reasons of the heart.

1. Which of the factors listed below motivate you to say yes to adding something to your schedule? Check all that apply.

   ☐ I like activity and being with people.
   ☐ I enjoy serving others.
   ☐ I want to be a good steward of the gifts God has given me.
   ☐ I don't like to spend a lot of time alone.
   ☐ I say yes to things God is clearly leading me into.
   ☐ I say yes to activities that allow me to relate to close friends.
   ☐ Sometimes it seems I'm the only one who can do the job.
   ☐ I want the affirmation and acceptance of others.
   ☐ I don't like disappointing people by saying no.
   ☐ I feel guilty saying no to ministry activities.
   ☐ Other:

2. Does most of the pressure in your life come from yourself or from others? Explain.

D An Anatomy of Overcommitment

One common reason is overestimating. We think we can do more than we really can. At one level this poor judgment is a result of shortsightedness. At another level, failing to recognize our limitations flows out of wanting to deny that we have limitations.

In Christian circles we sometimes compound the problem by assuming that God will guard us from foolishness, especially if we are doing His work. So we see the specter of pious workaholics, creeping ever closer to disaster, preferring to "burn out rather than rust out for Jesus." Wanting to be a bit more than human, we modestly slip into a phone booth, don our superhero outfit, and try to leap tall buildings with a single bound! After a building or two, the spring goes out of our legs and we fall from the sky and start crashing into things, discovering the sober fact that we have limits.

We also trap ourselves with pleasing. We say yes to please other people—to make sure they'll like us. We people pleasers can sniff out even the slightest hint of anger or disappointment, and this acute sense triggers a yes to fend it off. Pleasers are especially inclined to fall for invitations decorated by phrases like, "You know, I think you're terrific at . . . ," or "It would really make me happy if you . . ." Of course, there is nothing wrong with wanting to be accepted or to feel worthy. But when it gets out of balance, our need for acceptance tyrannizes us and leads us into wrong choices. We mustn't say yes just to please.

3. Romans 12:3 says, "Do not think of yourself more highly than you ought, but rather think of yourself with sober judgment, in accordance with the measure of faith God has given you." What do you think it means to "think of yourself with sober judgment"?

4. How might thinking "of yourself more highly than you ought" lead to overcommitment?

5. Describe your capacity for work and activity.

6. What kinds of activities are particularly draining for you?

7. How much time do you need to rest and recharge?

8. How frequently do you bite off more than you can chew by overestimating your capacity?

9. What kinds of problems might be created by denying our God-given limitations?

10. Another reason we sometimes say yes to the wrong things is to please others. Record what the following Scriptures say.

   ▪ John 5:30

   ▪ 1 Corinthians 4:3

   ▪ Galatians 1:10

   ▪ Ephesians 5:10

   ▪ 1 Thessalonians 2:4

11. Based on the verses you just read, what was the primary motivation in the ministries of Jesus and of Paul?

12. Why do you think Paul says that desiring to please men and be a servant of Christ are incompatible goals?

13. On a scale of 1 to 10 (1 = rarely, 10 = frequently), how often do you do things that are primarily motivated by a desire to please others?

D To the Rescue

Similar to pleasing is rescuing, a reason of the heart closely akin to pride. Here the invitation usually comes in the form, "I don't think we can do without you," or "You're the only one who can . . . ," or "You're exactly the person we need." The whole enterprise, we are told, will rise or fall depending on what we do. What a feast for our pride! A little adrenaline rush urges us to don a white hat, strap on a gun belt full of silver bullets, and gallop off to rescue the belea- guered and distressed. After all, it's not every day you get to be a messiah.

Sometimes in frustration we even do this to ourselves. "Somebody has to do something!" we complain and then add, "And because nobody else seems to be getting the job done, I guess that somebody will have to be me."

Rescuing has power over us because the need seems so des- perate and the resources, apart from our own, seem so few. But we would do well to remember who the Messiah really is and to observe a few cautions.

First, even when those who plead with us are sincere in saying that we're the only ones who can do it, they're often wrong. They may not have thought creatively enough to discover solutions equally as good or even better. Second, just because they're desperate doesn't mean it's our responsibility. And even if disaster strikes, it doesn't mean it's our fault. Finally, we need to ask ourselves who among those pressing us for our help will come to rescue us, the rescuers, from ourselves. When we regard the flattery of others and our own pride, we pay a dear price.

14. Sometimes we say yes because we—or others—believe that we're the only person who can do a particular job. While there may be a few rare situations where this is true, what else might this mind set reflect?

15. Read Deuteronomy 8:11-20. What does this passage say about the roots of our pride?

16. Why do you think confidence in our own abilities sometimes causes us to forget God?

17. Are there any situations in your life right now in which it appears to you (or someone else) that you are the only person who can accomplish a given task? Spend some time brainstorming other possible solutions—including other people who might be able to help.

D Goaded by Guilt

We also say yes instead of no when we are driven by guilt or a sense of duty. There are duties that are properly ours, and we deserve the guilt we feel when we fail in them. But just as surely, there are duties that are not ours, and we need to know the difference. Often I'm tempted to feel guilty, when for example, others urge me to share the passion they have for particular causes—wonderful causes for the most part. Missions. Evangelism. Ministry to the elderly, youth, the homeless, substance abusers, the hungry, orphans, or the imprisoned. Sunday school teaching. The church choir. Work for peace and justice. Those who are called and committed to God's work in these areas all seem to want me to commit myself in the same way, and some would even shame me into it. Even though it's impossible to be passionate about everything, I often feel guilt anyway.

I'm also tempted to feel guilty about taking care of my needs when others want me to help with their needs. Out of guilt we're tempted to slight our own needs for rest, recreation, study, prayer, and other disciplines of a well-ordered life.

Sometimes we're made to feel guilty by those who think that, in some way, we're in their debt. At times we do "owe" others our time and strength. But I suspect it is much less often than they would suggest.

18. What are some circumstances in your life that can create guilt, as described by the author?

19. Read Luke 4:42-43. What can we learn from Jesus about declining the demands others sometimes place on us?

D Saying Yes to No

Fortunately, although it may have a strong grip on us, we need not be trapped by the dilemma of yes and no.

We can learn, for example, to honor our limits. We can accept the reality of limitation. The truth is that we can neither respond to every need nor accept every invitation. So the practical question is not whether we will draw the line, but where we will draw the line.

I receive many appeals in the mail for donations to charity, mission, educational, and relief organizations. Most of these organizations are worthy, most of the appeals urgent. I would like to respond to them all, generously if I could. But my bank and creditors would soon object if I did because I would soon spend all the money I have. Our time and energies have similar limits. Let's make sure we're not spending them into deep debt.

Another practical step is to know and honor our place. Part of God's mercy to us is our uniqueness. We each have particular gifts and a place to fill. Paul made this point when he taught the church about varieties of gifts and diverse parts of the body (Romans 12, 1 Corinthians 12, Ephesians 4). The beauty of this plan is that each of us is entrusted with important tasks while none of us is required to do everything. We only need to know our place and be obedient to what it requires. We don't even need to guarantee the results of our obedience because only God can do that anyway.

---

20. Read 1 Corinthians 12, paying attention to the discussion of roles. How might understanding our place in the body of Christ help keep us from taking on too much responsibility?

21. How do you think pride distorts our perspective on our capabilities and the way we see others' contributions?

I've also found it helpful to take time to give time. Instead of accepting an invitation as soon as it comes, I usually insist on time to think about it before responding. I'll say, "If you must have an answer now, I'll have to say no. If you can wait and want me to think and pray about it, I'll be happy to consider it." Often I will ask the person to put the request in writing, including as much relevant detail as possible. Refusing to give an answer on the spot helps deliver me from both the pressure of others and the enticements of my own spirit. It also gives me a chance to think carefully, to pray about it, and to consult with trusted advisers who help guard me from myself. Through both success and failure I've learned that a thoughtful answer is better than an instant yes.

To know when to say yes or no, we also need to calculate more accurately what various activities cost us in time, money, and energy. If we pay attention, we can learn from our experience and from the experience of others. I've been learning what is required to accept an out-of-town speaking engagement—from the preparation and details involved before the trip to the energies spent on catching up once I get home. It's a lot more than I would have guessed. Similarly, when someone asks us to serve on a committee or participate in a project, we would be wise to ask what it costs from someone who has already done that task.

One part of counting the cost is to recognize what we are saying no to when we say yes. If we do some things, we will not be able to do others. We can ask ourselves, "If I say yes, am I silently saying no to other things that matter to me? To my family? To study or rest? To solitude? To others that I'm called to serve?" Every yes hides a no, and we would do well to flush it out into the open.

Once we have finally decided, we can then rest joyfully in God. We don't need to stir up the decision-making process with regrets that we can't do whatever we've chosen against. Instead, we can delight in having made as wise and obedient a decision as we know how. We mustn't fret over whether others will succeed without us, whether we would be blamed if they don't, or whether they might succeed and we weren't essential after all.

And we can relax. We don't need to bear the burden of making the right decision all of the time. We'll make mistakes. But we can listen as well as we can, be as obedient as we can, and move on.

22. In Luke 14:28-33, Jesus told two parables about the importance of counting the cost. What are the consequences of failing to count the cost?

23. How well do you "count the cost" of your obligations?

   ☐ I usually underestimate the work, energy, and time needed.
   ☐ Most of the time I'm a good judge of what they will cost.
   ☐ I often overestimate the time and energy a project will take.
   ☐ Other:

24. What is the "cost" of your level of busyness? What things are you unable to do that you would like to do—or that you feel are important to do?

25. Review the motivations for saying yes we've highlighted in this session. To which are you most susceptible? How can you use this knowledge the next time you face a potential commitment?

3

Two Views on Setting Priorities Biblically

As we try to get a grip on busyness, one important question we must answer is "What really matters?" How do we identify what is a priority and what isn't? While the question is a simple one, many well-meaning voices in our society answer it differently. Even within Christian circles there exists a diverse range of opinions about what matters the most. As you read through the two articles that follow, entitled **"God First, Family Second . . . Right?" by Doug Sherman** (excerpted from Issue 60), and **"The Myth of the Balanced Life" by Paul Stanley** (excerpted from Issue 60), pay close attention to the two different approaches to setting priorities. Then move on to the questions and exercises that follow.

GOD FIRST, FAMILY SECOND . . . RIGHT?

If you have been to a few Christian conferences, read a few Christian books, or listened to at least thirty sermons in the past year, you may have developed a picture of the "committed Christian life" that looks something like this: study the Bible daily for an hour, pray daily for an hour, lead devotions with your children each night, share Christ with an unbeliever twice a week, attend church twice a week, teach Sunday school or serve on a church committee, and participate in a community service project. Of course the yard is mowed, the house is cleaned, a job is performed, meals are cooked, and quality time is spent with friends.

The profile is a composite of messages from well-meaning Christian teachers, but it reflects a view of life from an earlier era. The Bureau of Labor Statistics reports that 90 percent of all couples have two incomes, and 67 percent of all mothers with children under the age of 18 work.

How can we live in obedience to God as our free time diminishes and the demands on it increase? One system for organizing responsibilities has become popular in some Christian circles. It goes something like this: God first, family second, church third, work and friends fourth. This "ladder of priorities" was derived from some of the discipleship passages about Christ having our supreme loyalty. But do these passages really advocate such a priority system? I don't think so. Let me explain.

First, Christ is to have first place in all areas of life (Colossians 1:18). He is to be the Lord of our work, our families, and all other areas. Putting God first and the other areas second implies that He is not a vital part of the other areas.

Second, most of life is not comprised of *either/or* but *both/and* situations. Rarely does life give us the choice, Am I going to be a good parent or a good worker? We must do both, with some measure of success.

Third, the ladder approach doesn't consider necessary tradeoffs. For example, if my church wants me to take on additional responsibility, how would this ladder approach help? Instead it leaves many followers of Christ feeling that no matter how fast they pedal, they're not pedaling fast enough.

Finally, when we put work on the lowest rung of the ladder we imply that work is a lower form of the Christian life. This is simply not the case. Your work matters as much to God as the work of your pastor or missionary. Legitimate work meets needs that He wants to meet through you.

---

1.   What are the main priorities in your life at the moment?

2.   Describe how you currently set priorities and make decisions.

3.   How effectively does this enable you to manage or juggle
     your priorities?

D The Christian Pentathlon

A helpful way of organizing life is to compare it to a pentathlon—
one of Europe's most prestigious athletic events.

The pentathlon requires the athlete to be proficient in five
areas: pistol shooting, fencing, horseback riding, swimming, and
running. It involves a wide range of skills and knowledge and
requires a thoughtful strategy for training. The athletes' training
time must be carefully divided among the events, although some
events will take longer to train for than others. The goal is to do
well in all areas to win the prize.

The Christian life is similar to the pentathlon. As I have studied
the apostle Paul's letter to the Romans and his other epistles, I have
identified five important areas of the Christian life: church, community, personal life, family, and work. There are many passages in the
epistles and throughout the New Testament that speak about those
areas, a few of which are listed below.

- *Church*: Romans 12:3-21, 14:1-23, Ephesians 4:1-16
- *Community*: Romans 13:1-14, Colossians 4:5-6
- *Personal Life*: Romans 12:1-2, Ephesians 4:17–5:21, 6:10-20,
  Colossians 3:1-17
- *Family*: Ephesians 5:22–6:4, Colossians 3:18-21
- *Work*: Ephesians 6:5-9, Colossians 3:22–4:1

Sherman identifies a number of passages that deal with the five spheres of responsibility in the Christian pentathlon. One long section of the book of Ephesians covers four of the five areas. Read through Ephesians 4:1–6:12 and answer the following questions.

4. As you read Paul's description of Christian responsibility (church, personal life, family, and work), do you get a sense that one area is more important than another? Why is that significant?

Now let's look specifically at each of these four areas, in the order in which they appear in Ephesians.

Ephesians 4:1-16: Serving in the Church

5. For what purpose has God given gifts to each believer?

6. Look at the lists of gifts Paul describes in verses 11-12, and in 1 Corinthians 12:8-10,28. If you have never thought much about your spiritual gifts and are not sure what they are, think about the gifts listed in these verses and consider what your gifts might be.

7. Do your current activities use the spiritual gifts God has given you?

8. Engaging in activities for which you are not well-suited or gifted can contribute to a "too busy" lifestyle. If your commitments fall outside of your primary areas of gifting, consider the following two questions:

- Are there roles in the church, other than the areas in which you're now serving, that are more in line with your gifting?

- Are you doing things for which others in the body might be more gifted?

Ephesians 5:1-21: Your Personal Life

9. Paul admonishes us to "be very careful, then, how you live . . . making the most of every opportunity" (verses 15-16). How might excessive busyness affect your ability to live carefully and make the most of every opportunity?

Ephesians 5:22–6:4: Family

10. What responsibilities does Paul define in this passage for each of the following?

- Wives

- Husbands

- Children

- Fathers

11.   How does the overall level of activity in your life affect your ability to fulfill these familial responsibilities?

Ephesians 6:5-9: Work

12.   How much does your job contribute to busyness in your life? (For example: *I work forty hours a week and am able to get my work done and not think about it much once I am away from work. Or I frequently put in overtime that adds stress to my life and makes it more difficult to fulfill my other obligations.*)

13.   Paul talks about serving "wholeheartedly, as if you were serving the Lord, not men" (verse 7). Does this describe your attitude at work? How might your level of busyness interfere with your ability to do your job this way?

14. a. The author identifies community as a component of the Christian pentathlon. Read Esther 10:3 and write down some ways in which a person might work "for the good of his people."

b. How might extreme busyness affect one's ability or inclination to be involved in community issues?

D Given the range of possibilities we have and the limited time in a day, tradeoffs are necessary. Nevertheless, the goal of the believer is to improve and be more Christlike in each area.

Although the pentathlon analogy is limited and imperfect, we can gain new perspective by viewing the Christian life in this way. The pentathlon approach . . .

- demonstrates that the Christian life is one unified whole of serving Christ
- offers an active view of the Christian life and encourages us to improve our habits, analyze our motives, and nurture our relationships
- provides a more realistic way to view our responsibilities
- underscores that our best is good enough and that God values progress, not perfection
- offers a radically different view of life from the way our culture sees it

Living in a society that puts a premium on career achievement tempts us to give little thought to pleasing the Lord in our non-work responsibilities. However, it may take just as much thought and planning to have a good marriage as it does to have a good career. It may take as much thought and prayer to develop a love for Christ as it does to map out your next job choice.

The pentathlon approach encourages us to inventory all areas of life so that we don't overtrain in one area to the detriment of another. For example, if I am too busy at church to be a godly parent, maybe the solution is to give up my position on the XYZ committee. Just as the pentathlete has a strategy for training to excel in five areas, the Christian needs a strategy that promotes progress and achieves a measure of balance for each area of life.

If you are serious about bringing your life into balance, take some time—a few hours or a day—to get away from the phone and your responsibilities to think prayerfully.

Consider your life against the framework of the five suggested categories. In what areas are you strong? What areas need improvement? Ask God to point out imbalance, particularly if one area is limiting your faithfulness to God in other areas. After this inventory, perhaps you will feel led to cut back in one area in order to bolster another.

Second, look at the progress you are making in each area. You might want to set a goal to increase your progress and to cultivate more faithfulness to Christ in each area.

Third, accept God's sovereignty over your life and over the time at your disposal. There is just enough time in every day to do what He wants. This does not mean you will accomplish everything you want to accomplish. It does mean that when your head touches the pillow at night you can feel settled in your spirit that you have worked hard to honor God with the time and responsibilities He gave you.

15. Reflect on the author's questions in the preceding paragraphs. In which areas are you strong right now? In which do you need improvement?

16. Sometimes we try to make many adjustments to our lives at once in an all-out effort to address the weaknesses we see. Often these self-improvement blitzes fail because we're focusing our efforts in too many directions. Look at the areas you identified as needing improvement in question 15. Which area is most in need of attention? What *one* change can you begin to make today to address this area of weakness?

The Myth of the Balanced Life

I've met believers who are models of the "balanced life."

Their giving flows out of a beautifully balanced budget, and their lifestyles include all the right activities to develop balance. Their priorities undergo tough appraisal to ensure they are "properly" weighted. Even their service to Christ is balanced to carefully include "enough but not too much."

But I wonder: Are people who strive for balance in their lives following Christ, or a value system concocted by the elusive "experts"? Have we elevated balance to a place never intended in Scripture?

Under the commonly held concept of the balanced life, Jesus was often out of balance. He missed meals, worked long hours, and seemed to have many short nights. We find Jesus getting up early to pray when He probably could have used the sleep (Mark 1:35). He even spent forty days praying and fasting, to the point that angels had to minister to Him.

Yet as we read through the Gospels, we don't get the impression that Jesus was always pressing Himself and His disciples to the outer limits, continually neglecting physical rest and nourishment.

How did Jesus decide when it was time to minister and when to rest? His statement in John 4 gives us a clue.

Jesus and His disciples, on the way from Judea to Galilee, were tired and hungry when they stopped in a small Samaritan village. Yet Jesus set aside His needs in order to lead an adulterous Samaritan woman to the Living Water. As His disciples joined Him by the town well, they were concerned about His need to eat, but He wasn't. Christ responded, "My food . . . is to do the will of him who sent me and to finish his work" (John 4:34).

Jesus determined when to eat and when to abstain, when to work and when to rest by seeking His Father's guidance. Christ's drive was not to achieve balance, but to do the will of the Father.

17. The idea that life should be in balance is a common one. What is your initial reaction to the author's challenge of this assumption?

18. How does Stanley's approach to establishing priorities and making decisions in this article differ from the Christian pentathlon described by Sherman in the preceding article?

19. After reading John 5:19 and John 8:28, how would you describe the way Jesus set priorities and made decisions? (Note: In session five we will further explore the subject of making decisions as Jesus did.)

D Out of Control

Sensitivity to the Holy Spirit, not a preconceived yardstick, must determine our priorities as well. The goal in life is never balance but rather doing God's will to the fullest, with all the energy and time He gives us. Like Jesus, we, too, will sometimes devote a disproportionate amount of time and energy to one area as we listen to and obey His Spirit.

God never intended for us to live balanced lives, with all aspects under control. While we may prefer to live within self-defined boundaries that allow us to be safe and in control, following Christ more often requires risk. We need to be willing to be out of balance so Christ can lead us where He wants us.

Faith begins to grow when we sacrifice something in our monthly budget to give a little more than last month, especially when it's focused on a need the Spirit has revealed. Dependence on Christ's power meets blessing when we step beyond our comfort zone and give time and love to people around us . . . even when it takes resources we may not think we have or time we've intended to devote elsewhere. It seems that most of the work of the kingdom is done by overworked believers with average gifts and few earthly resources. Perhaps these laborers don't know about balance yet.

20.   Is having life "under control" a goal that Christians should pursue? Why or why not?

D Whose Agenda?

Spending years with Eastern European and Russian believers changed my life in the area of balance. They were always out of balance by anyone's measure. Food supplies were erratic, persecution was unpredictable, and change was constant. As a result, they did not worry about tomorrow but focused on fulfilling God's will today. They knew He would take care of the rest.

And He did! None of them ever starved (though they often ate a lot of one food). They had adequate clothing. But most of all, God was powerfully working in and through them. Always giving and sharing, these believers saw God answer prayer, change lives, and fulfill promises.

The apostle Paul challenged the Ephesians to live wisely, "making the most of every opportunity"; not to be foolish, but to "understand what the Lord's will is" (Ephesians 5:15-18). If we worry and think too much about balance, it is easy to fall into an agenda that stifles the Spirit's prompting.

Somehow, we must trust that God is at work in us and that the way He is moving in our lives is part of a larger movement in the world. As we respond to His Spirit, God reveals to us the steps we are to take toward fulfilling His will . . . and this may pull our lives out of balance. Very often it is in these out-of-balance times and circumstances that God teaches us new and vital lessons because He has our attention. After all, when do we call upon the "Wonderful Counselor, Mighty God, Everlasting Father, and Prince of Peace"? When we are out of balance. He also works through us because our faith is alive and we are thrust into dependence upon Him (2 Corinthians 12:10). His power shows up best in weak people.

Let's model our lives after those who have followed Christ in the New Testament. They were abandoned to God's will at any cost and allowed God the freedom to pull them out of balance anytime. As a matter of fact, they anticipated it. Most of their lives were spent drawing upon Christ in their "out-of-balance-yet-in-His-will" state. True growth and adventure with Christ takes place in out of balance living.

21. How do you think seeking balance might "stifle the Spirit's prompting"?

22. Sherman's approach to living a life that pleases God is based on wisely evaluating how we're doing in areas that the Scriptures teach are important. Stanley's approach rests on being attentive to the Spirit's leading. Are Sherman and Stanley's conceptions exclusive of one another? Why or why not?

Words Worth Remembering

But to what must we be committed? To Jesus Christ Himself— to be in love not with a cause, but with the One who gives us the cause.

—Bob Boardman, from "A Call to Commitment," Issue 2

4

Taking Stock

1. In the study thus far, what has been the most encouraging quote or passage of Scripture? How has it encouraged you?

2. What are you still discouraged about in your battle against busyness?

3. What has been the most significant change you've made in your life so far as a result of your study?

Session One: An Easy Yoke?

4. Go back to session one, question 8, on page 11, and look again at the picture of your yoke and the attached cart. Has your perspective on your yoke changed since you began this study? (For example: *I didn't realize how much I was over-estimating my capacity. I can see more clearly now that my yoke was killing me.*)

5. If your yoke is too heavy, what adjustments have you begun to make?

6. a. In his article "Take a Load Off," David Henderson says we can take on Christ's easy yoke by making ourselves open and available to God and by building in time for reflection. What is the single biggest obstacle in your life to spending time with God regularly?

b. Take some time to think about what specific changes you would need to make in order to overcome that obstacle. Then complete the following sentence: To overcome this obstacle to spending regular time with God, I will . . .

7. a. Read Matthew 11:28-30 again.

"Come to me, all you who are weary and burdened, and I will give you rest. Take my yoke upon you and learn from me, for I am gentle and humble in heart, and you will find rest for your souls. For my yoke is easy and my burden is light."

b. This promise of rest and an easy yoke must be claimed in faith. Often we're encouraged by a promise such as this, yet wonder if we can really experience it. One way we can begin to respond in faith to such a promise is to pray through it. In the space on the next page, write your own prayer of response to Jesus' promise of rest. There is no right or wrong way to do this. The important thing is to respond honestly to Jesus' words even as you ask Him to make this promise a reality in your life. (The following paragraph is an example of what such a prayer might look like.)

Jesus, I thank You that You've promised me rest. I thank You that You know I'm tired and that You want me to come to You. But as hard as I try, Lord, I just can't seem to find the rest You're talking about. I want to believe, but I'm frustrated that I just don't feel like I'm experiencing an easy yoke. I keep saying yes to things for the wrong reasons, even when I know I should say no. Lord, too often I want to please others, not You. Too often I'm afraid of what others will think of me if I turn them down. Jesus, I believe You want me to know the rest You've promised, but it seems

41

like I make a lot of mistakes that keep it from happening. Lord, I pray that You will help me to enter into the rest You promise. I want to learn from You, as You've promised. Give me the wisdom and courage to make the right decisions. Help me to know when I need to cease striving and just sit at Your feet. Help me not to give up, but to keep coming to You. Thank You for Your goodness, Jesus. Amen.

Session Two: Why Am I So Busy?

8. In his article "Just Say No," Howard R. Macy identified a number of reasons we accept responsibility and make commitments when we should say no. Check any of these reasons that apply to you.

☐ Overestimating
☐ Pleasing
☐ Rescuing
☐ Guilt
☐ Other:

9. In the chart on the next page, list each of your current commitments. Next to it record your primary motivation for taking on this obligation (there was a need, you felt you would be using your gifts, and so on). An example is given.

Commitment	Motivation
Leading our Bible study	I was the only equipped person available.

10. Are there any patterns evident in your motivations? Are you more susceptible to some reasons for saying yes than to others?

11. Which activities are motivated by questionable or negative factors?

12. Did you discover any other motivations for involvement not previously discussed in this session? If so, what were they?

13. In what areas of your life do you tend to struggle with your limitations? Check all that apply.

   ☐ Rest (not getting enough sleep)
   ☐ Physical capacity (frequent bouts of exhaustion)
   ☐ Eating habits (overeating, skipping meals, eating most meals at restaurants)
   ☐ Budgeting and spending habits (money or time)
   ☐ Social/ministry engagements (overcommitting)
   ☐ Responsibilities (accepting large work or ministry assignments when life is already hectic)
   ☐ Other:

14. If you're exceeding your limitations, what is one thing you can do today to begin to acknowledge and live within your limits?

15. When we understand our limitations and motivations, we're better able to say no to opportunities that may not be the best for us. Two important biblical truths can help free us from pressure to please others, from performing out of duty, or from feeling guilty: God loves us and He is sovereign. Read the passages below and answer the questions that follow.

   "I am God, and there is no other; I am God, and there is none like me. I make known the end from the beginning, from ancient times, what is still to come. I say: My purpose will stand, and I will do all that I please." (Isaiah 46:9-10)

   For by him all things were created: things in heaven and on earth, visible and invisible, whether thrones or powers or rulers or authorities; all things were created by him and for him. He is before all things, and in him all things hold together.

And, he is the head of the body, the church; he is the beginning and the firstborn from among the dead, so that in everything he might have the supremacy. (Colossians 1:16-18)

16. Circle the words and phrases from these passages that describe God's sovereignty and power.

17. What do these passages teach about God's ability to accomplish His purposes?

18. How do these passages challenge us when we think we're indispensable?

19. The author indicates that we may say yes because we think we need to earn our worth in God's eyes or the eyes of others. Read the passages below and answer the questions that follow.

The LORD your God is with you, he is mighty to save. He will take great delight in you, he will quiet you with his love, he will rejoice over you with singing. (Zephaniah 3:17)

I no longer call you servants, because a servant does not know his master's business. Instead, I have called you friends. (John 15:15)

Therefore, there is now no condemnation for those who are in Christ Jesus. (Romans 8:1)

But he [Jesus] said to me, "My grace is sufficient for you, for my power is made perfect in weakness." (2 Corinthians 12:9)

20. Circle the words that describe the love God has for us, and the kind of relationship we now have with God.

21. How do you think remembering God's love for you might help you say no in the future?

Session Three: Two Views on Setting Priorities Biblically

22. Think back over the last month of your life. How have you invested time and energy in each of the five areas of the Christian pentathlon?

    - Church

    - Community

    - Personal life

    - Family

    - Work

23. In his article "God First, Family Second . . . Right?" Doug Sherman talks about the importance of training to compete well in multiple events. What purpose does training serve in the life of an athlete?

24. What kinds of things does an athlete's training usually consist of?

25. Paul compared the Christian life to a demanding race (read 1 Corinthians 9:24-27). What is the purpose of the strict training Paul describes?

26. How do you think the discipline of training helps someone focus on his or her priorities?

27. Pick one of the five areas of the Christian pentathlon in which you feel you're weak. Brainstorm some "training exercises" that would help strengthen you in this area.

- Chapter 1 An Easy yoke. Read pg 7 We discussed that the rest is not necessarily physical rest but mental rest

- Chapter 2 We talked about why we are so busy

- Chapter 3 We talked about setting priorities. What is important and what is not important. What really matters

- Read quote from above
- The question remains how do we make decisions in our life in using our time. commitments and resource

How many of us make decisions in a vacuum with no input from others?

— Give example of how "Teams" are utilized at work for making major decision or working on complex problems

Discerning God's Voice as We Make Decisions

In session three, we examined two ways to set priorities. The second article in that session focused on the way Jesus made decisions. This session will continue to build on some of those ideas.

1. A number of factors can influence our thinking as we make choices. On which of the following do you rely as you seek God's will in a particular decision? Check all that apply.

   ☐ God's Word
   ☐ Circumstances
   ☐ "Doors" that are clearly open   OR CLOSED
   ☐ The counsel of others
   ☐ Your own wisdom, common sense, and thoughts on the matter
   ☐ God's clear leading through an inner voice, impression, or conviction
   ☐ Your own desires in the situation
   ☐ Other:

   DOES ANYONE HAVE AN EXAMPLE?

2.   Consider a recent decision you made in which you were initially uncertain of God's will. Describe the things God used to lead you through that process. (For example: *He used a verse to challenge me to consider getting involved in a new ministry*.)

As we consider the relationships and activities that make our lives busy, we must pause to ask the question, "What does God want me to do?" Beating busyness depends upon hearing from God about our myriad obligations. Are they all equally important from His perspective? Looking at them through the lens of His expressed priorities, do they all deserve a place in our lives? In the following article, entitled **"The Sound of His Voice" by Judith Couchman** (excerpted from Issue 108), we'll explore several biblical benchmarks for learning how to discern God's voice.

D THE SOUND OF HIS VOICE

As a young Christian, I asked this question many times, and I seldom received a workable answer. In the Bible, God's voice traveled a range of volumes and intensities, depending on the situation. He thundered when defending His people (Psalm 18:13). After a windstorm, earthquake, and fire, He whispered to Elijah at the mouth of an isolated cave (1 Kings 19:11-13). But what would be the nature of His voice if He spoke to me personally, in the recesses of my heart? I've had to answer that question myself and be willing to wait, listen, and, more often than not, learn from my blunders.

In one sense, we all have to identify God's voice by ourselves. He speaks uniquely to each of us, and from experience we learn whether we're hearing our own imagination or even the Devil's deceptive voice. At the same time, it helps to learn how other believers discern His voice and what prompts them to act on what they've heard. So in the past few months I've conducted an experiment. When people have said, "God told me . . . ," I've asked,

"How do you know He told you?" The answers have varied. Some people sputtered vague explanations and couldn't offer concrete descriptions. Others described specific signposts and feelings that identified God's voice to them.

3. One of the difficulties of hearing God's voice is distinguishing it from other voices that might be speaking to us as well. What other potential voices does the author identify?

4. Read 1 Samuel 3:1-10. In this passage, God calls Samuel, but Samuel doesn't recognize His voice. How did Samuel learn to recognize God's voice?

HE UNDERSTOOD FROM ELI   VS. 9

As you continue reading, keep in mind that learning to recognize God's voice is a process, just as it was for Samuel. Later in this session we'll take a look at the ways God confirms His leading through other means of guidance.

D Heart and Mind

From my experience, a two-pronged pattern seems common. Sometimes the Holy Spirit impresses a thought upon our minds; sometimes He stirs our hearts. If He speaks to the mind, it's usually a thought that intrudes upon the brain and is markedly different from what we've been thinking about. It possesses a distinct quality that causes us to say, "I wouldn't have considered that myself!" and suddenly gives us enlightenment into people or situations. If the Spirit speaks to the heart, it's often through a nudge that compels us to action, or a sense of restraint that warns us not to move forward. The mind and heart can also sync, with a thought that agrees with an inner impression. Lest this all sounds too ethereal, I'll share some everyday examples.

After fifteen years of hardy service, my Ford Escort finally needed to retire, so I sold it for a pittance and purchased a new vehicle. What a change! I hadn't realized how smoothly and swiftly a vehicle could travel.

In the first month, however, the "swiftly" aspect got me into trouble. In a hurry to attend a meeting, I picked up speed on a stretch near my home, and a policeman's radar clocked me at ten miles an hour over the limit. *I'm not a speeder,* I thought. But the ticket—and seventy-five-dollar fine—disagreed with me.

For the next several months I carefully monitored my speedometer. One day, however, as I drove toward that same neighborhood, a voice inside said, *Go home.* "That's a weird thought," I muttered to myself. *Go home,* it said again. But I didn't listen.

An hour later the same policeman again clocked me at ten miles an hour over the limit. This time the ticket doubled to $150.

"Oh, Lord," I sighed, "what are You trying to teach me?" I expected an intensely spiritual answer like "absolute obedience" or "continual brokenness."

Instead, these words crossed my brain: *Slow down.*

At times, God's messages are simply pragmatic. Since then I've realized that, yes, I do tend to speed. It wasn't the new vehicle, it was me, and I needed to change.

Another incident, still fresh in my mind after eighteen years, first taught me about God's warnings expressed as inner reservations. At the time, a man moved into the apartment across the hall from me. He was amiable, spiritually inclined, and we often talked in the stairwell. "You ought to visit my church sometime," he told me.

"Okay," I said without thinking. But internally I felt as though an alarm had sounded. After that, each time we chatted I felt a jarring within, or what some people call a "check" in my spirit.

I never attended church with the man, and I later discovered he belonged to a cult. When I found out, I immediately recognized that God had warned and most likely protected me from something spiritually harmful.

5. The author describes two ways God commonly speaks to
    believers: through a specific thought in our minds and
    through a "check," or strong impression, in our spirit that we
    should or shouldn't do something. How have you experi-
    enced God's guidance through these means in your life?

6. Have you ever acted contrary to what you suspected to be
    God's leading, as in the author's example above? What were
    the consequences?

Discerning His Voice

However God speaks to our souls—in our quiet times of reading
and prayer, in the hum of a scheduled day—there are some guiding
characteristics by which we can discern whether an inner message
is from Him. Keep in mind, though, that we can't fit God into a for-
mula to always predict how He will communicate with us.
Consequently, these guidelines are not etched-in-stone rules.

God speaks with clarity. "His sheep follow him because they
know his voice" (John 10:4). Over time we learn to recognize the
quality of God's voice and how He sounds to us. We can be assured,
though, that He doesn't speak in fuzzy generalities. If the message is
muddled, we probably need to wait until the communication clari-
fies. God's voice and messages are clear. Though we may need to
wait for the Lord's confirmation, often when He speaks, we know
He has spoken to us.

For a time, God may stir our hearts with a general sense that
"something's up" and a change of direction is forthcoming. This

holy restlessness causes us to seek God's will and prepares our hearts for His message. When He finally speaks, it's with clarity. We transition from "I think God might be speaking to me" to "I know that He spoke to me."

✱   God's voice is specific. "Whether you turn to the right or to the left, your ears will hear a voice behind you, saying, 'This is the way; walk in it'" (Isaiah 30:21). The specificity of God's message relates closely to the clarity of His voice, and often the two characteristics are so intertwined they can't be separated.

---

7. The author says, "Often when He speaks, we know He has spoken to us." Do you agree with this, or do you sometimes question whether you've actually heard from God?

8. a. As you read the following passages, jot down the phrases related to hearing God when He speaks to us.

   ▪ Deuteronomy 30:19-20

   LISTEN TO HIS VOICE

   ▪ Isaiah 30:21

   YOUR EAR WILL HEAR A VOICE

   ▪ John 10:2-4

   THE SHEEP LISTEN TO HIS VOICE · HE CALLS THEM BY NAME

   ▪ John 16:13-14

   He will speak only what he hears and he will tell you what is yet to come

   b. What do these verses teach about God's desire to guide us through His voice?

ISA 30:21 This is the way. Walk in it
God wants us to know the way

54

c. What do these passages say about our ability to discern God's voice?

As sheep listen to their shepard, so should we listen to God's voice and understand

9. What kinds of things does God promise to those who listen to Him?

D **God is not in a hurry.** Second Peter 3:8 tells us, "But do not forget this one thing, dear friends: With the Lord a day is like a thousand years, and a thousand years are like a day."

A bit of spiritual wisdom claims that God never runs, He walks. And like Enoch who "walked with God" (Genesis 5:22), He invites us to plod along with Him.

God confirms His message. Paul wrote, "For I tell you that Christ has become a servant of the Jews on behalf of God's truth, to confirm the promises made to the patriarchs" (Romans 15:8). If the Lord is leading us to move—or to stop moving—He usually speaks through several mouthpieces. For example, we may hear His voice within. Then someone delivers an unmistakably similar message to us. In our Bible reading, certain verses confirm what we've heard, and when we flip on the radio, a preacher is using that same passage as his text! Finally, when we explain the concept to trusted advisers, they agree that the message sounds like God's voice. In other words, when He's guiding us, God usually doesn't speak in a vacuum. He confirms His words so we're certain of His directive.

10. At the beginning of this session, we briefly considered some of the ways God guides us and confirms His leading as we make decisions. What do the verses below tell us about the variety of ways in which God does this?

a. His Word (2 Timothy 3:16, Hebrews 4:12-13)

Scripture is God Breathed
Word of God is living and active

b. Open doors or circumstances (Proverbs 16:9, 19:21; Romans 1:8-13)

Lord determines a mans steps
Ot is the Lords purpose that prevail
God to open the way

c. Counsel (Proverbs 11:14, 15:22)

many advisors make victory sure
Plans fail with lack of advisors

d. Wisdom (Proverbs 2:1-15)

understand the fear of the Lord and
find knowledge of God
understand what is right and just
Save you from the way of wicked

e. Our desires (Psalm 20:4, 21:2; Proverbs 10:24)

What the righteous desire will be grant
I give you the desires of your heart an
make all your plans succeed

D **God never contradicts His Word.** Psalm 111:7-8 says, "The works of his hands are faithful and just; all his precepts are trustworthy. They are steadfast for ever and ever, done in faithfulness and uprightness." Whatever God speaks to us, He will never contradict the truth of His precepts found in the Bible. Friends have said to me, "I have perfect peace about this," when their course of action obviously violated God's Word. (To be fair, I confess I've done this myself.) Peace is not an indicator of the Lord's approval or guidance if the underlying motive or action contradicts the Scriptures or leads us into sin. When we're seeking guidance or making a decision, nothing can supersede the Bible's holiness and authority.

So the guideline is simple: If the message runs contrary to the Scriptures, it's not God's voice. He will confirm with His Word, but never will He contradict it.

11. Read Romans 1:18-32. With this passage in mind, how is it possible to have "peace" about something that clearly violates God's Word?

VS 32 Although they knew Gods righteous decree, they not only continue to do these very things (sin) but also approve those who do them

12. Jesus said, "Whoever has my commands and obeys them, he is the one who loves me. He who loves me will be loved by my Father, and I too will love him and show myself to him" (John 14:21). What does this verse imply about the relationship between obedience and hearing God's voice?

Those who love God will follow and obey His commands and God will thus show Himself to him

START TODAY

D God's voice corrects instead of accuses. Paul wrote, "Therefore, there is now no condemnation for those who are in Christ Jesus" (Romans 8:1). If we're walking with God, when the Holy Spirit speaks He may reveal or convict us of our sin, but He doesn't accuse us. If the voice we hear is accusatory, it either belongs to the Devil (Revelation 12:10), ourselves, or someone other than God. Accusers shove us toward depression and destruction.

READ

Remember, too, that if God's voice does correct us, it is kind and cleansing, leading us to peace, healing, and joy.

God doesn't change His mind: "I the LORD do not change" (Malachi 3:6). Ever meet someone who says he's sure of God's will for him, but in a month he changes his mind? Then in a few more months he's certain it's something else? He probably hasn't heard from the Lord. When God calls us to a purpose or directs our steps, He doesn't career us first down one path and then down another. He accompanies us on a steady journey, even though at the moment the surrounding circumstances don't make sense.

All of these indicators of God's voice can be applied to the other ways we hear from Him: through the Scriptures, messengers, circumstances, and the supernatural. But few if any of these factors will aid our discernment if we don't nurture a tender heart. *WHY?*

To discern God's inner impression in the bustle of each day, we need to hide away with Him periodically, filling up on His presence and emptying out our sin, stress, and cluttered-up souls. Sitting at His feet, even if only for moments at a time, we learn to recognize His voice.

— READ

13. Read Hebrews 3:12-15. The author of Hebrews says that it's possible for us to recognize God's voice, yet harden our hearts to it. What factors in your life cause you to harden your heart toward God?

Sin, and unbelieving heart

Stubbornness

14. How do you think excessive busyness hardens our hearts toward God's voice?

We don't take the time to listen to His voice. God's voice will address our sins and unbelieving heart

58

15. What are some of the other things that make it difficult to hear God's voice?

Competing voices, taking time to listen. Don't want to hear

16. In the introduction to this article, the author said that she's learned to recognize God's voice by being "willing to wait, listen, and, more often than not, learn from my blunders." How is listening for God's leading in prayer different from simply voicing our requests or asking for guidance?

17. Is spending time before God listening for His direction an appealing idea or a threatening one? Explain your answer.

BOTH

Appealing — God loves His children and I will never forsake them
Threatening — He may lead us down a path of unknown

18. Listening to God is an act of surrender that expresses our dependence upon Him. For some, sitting quietly before God is a scary thing. What fears, if any, do you have about being silent before the Lord? Check all that apply.

□ I fear that God won't speak to me.
□ I worry that He won't have good things to say about me.
□ I fear God will ask me to do something I don't want to do.
□ I fear He's going to say no to something I want to do.
□ I'm afraid of being quiet with myself, let alone with God.
□ I fear I'll be unable to discern His voice, and might mistake my thoughts—or even Satan's voice—for His.
□ Other:

19. How do you think listening to God more carefully and frequently might affect the level of busyness in your life?

We need to slow down to listen to God's voice. Creating quiet times will slow us down

20. a. Sometime this week as you spend time with God, set aside a few minutes to actively listen to Him. If you've never done this before, start with a small block of time, perhaps five minutes. If you're wrestling with a particular decision, you might ask God to give you specific guidance. If you don't have any urgent decisions on your plate, simply ask Him to reveal Himself to you, then be quiet. If this exercise is a fearful one for any of the reasons listed above, tell God why it's difficult for you and ask Him to help you learn to listen anyway.

b. As you listen, God may bring specific things to mind, big or small. Or you may not hear much of anything. Having a notebook handy will enable you to record your impressions as you listen to Him. Write down anything that comes to mind.

Words Worth Remembering
All too often we . . . try to get God to tell us what He wants us to do so that we can decide whether we will do it.
— Steve Troxel, from "Taming Your Feelings," Issue 26

6

Writing a Personal Mission Statement

Another key to dealing with busyness is to clearly identify what God has called us to do. When we take the time to look closely at how God has created and led us, we can discover His purpose for our lives. A clear statement of our mission acts as a rudder in our lives when we're blown by the strong winds of incessant activity. A personal mission statement will help you to say yes and no with confidence to the multitude of choices you face. As you read through this session's article, entitled **"Put Your Purpose on Paper" by Freya Ottem Hanson** (excerpted from Issue 71), underline the ideas that stand out to you. Then move on to the questions and exercises that follow.

PUT YOUR PURPOSE ON PAPER

When I was a high school senior, I wrote a speech entitled "A Moral and Ethical Code for Teenagers." Although I wrote it hoping to win a college scholarship, it was to become much more than a way to fund my education.

In my speech I talked about living my life to please God rather than people. The last sentence was, "May my life be such that I live to bless mankind." Spoken more than twenty years ago, it has become my personal mission statement.

This goal has encouraged and challenged me in many areas of my life, particularly in my educational pursuits—first my undergraduate degree, and then my law degree. It also gave me the incentive to set up a law practice in a small town of two thousand people when my friends thought I was crazy for leaving the cosmopolitan life.

Would I have directed my life in these ways without a mission statement? I'm not sure; but I do know that by having a defined mission statement, I am living purposefully and with a sense of calling. How I continue to live out my mission statement is still evolving; yet over and over again it has pushed me in the direction of service to others.

Mission Accomplished

The Bible often reveals a personal mission statement for the men and women it portrays. Sometimes it even reveals the fulfillment of that mission. Scripture tells us that Jesus' sole mission was to accomplish the will of His Father. Jesus' words from the cross, "It is finished" (John 19:30), tell us that at His death the mission—God's provision for our salvation and restoration to Himself—was complete. The apostle Paul's mission was also concise and clear: "To carry my [Jesus'] name before the Gentiles and their kings and before the people of Israel" (Acts 9:15). Much later, Paul could state with confidence, "I have fought the good fight, I have finished the race, I have kept the faith" (2 Timothy 4:7).

Here are two other noteworthy mission statements mentioned in Scripture:

- John the Baptist: "I am the voice of one calling in the desert, 'Make straight the way for the Lord'" (John 1:23).
- The twelve disciples: "He sent them out to preach the kingdom of God and heal the sick" (Luke 10:1).

Each of these fulfilled their mission because it had been clearly articulated and they let it guide their actions.

1. Jesus often made statements that described His purpose on earth. Write down what the following verses reveal about His understanding of His mission.

   - Matthew 4:19   FOLLOW ME

   - Mark 10:45   HE CAME TO SERVE AND GIVE HIS LIFE

- Luke 4:43 *ANNOUNCE THE GOOD NEWS OF GOD'S KINGDOM*

- Luke 5:32

- Luke 18:31-33

- John 3:14-17

- John 6:38-39

- John 8:14,42

- John 9:39

2. What common ideas about His mission do you see repeated in these verses?

   DOING THE WILL OF THE FATHER

3. Paul, like Jesus, had a clear idea of what God had called him to do. Read the following passages and write down the main elements of Paul's mission from each.

   - Acts 9:15   *CARRY GOD'S NAME*

   - Romans 1:14-15   *PREACH THE GOSPILE*

   - 1 Corinthians 9:19   *SLAVE TO EVERYONE*

   - Ephesians 3:7-9

   - Philippians 3:10-11   *BECOME LIKE HIM IN DEATH*

   - Colossians 2:1-3   *SO THEY MAY KNOW THE TRUTH*

Why Have a Mission Statement?

A mission statement allows us to be guided by principles and beliefs. Too often we abandon ship when the going gets tough. Mission statements guide us at times we can't clearly see our way.

My own mission statement, drafted at the age of eighteen, encouraged me to stay in school even though I was tempted to quit. I knew that for me to serve others best, I needed an education. That guiding principle kept me struggling away at my law books at night while working a daytime job. It kept me from giving up when well-meaning friends would say, "Aren't you ever going to get done with school? You must be crazy to work that hard."

When fleeting moods, instead of principles and beliefs, control our mission, we're in danger of shipwreck.

A mission statement allows us to participate in something greater than ourselves. Before He ascended into heaven, Jesus gave His disciples a mission statement: "Go and make disciples of all nations, baptizing them . . . and teaching them to obey everything I have commanded you" (Matthew 28:19-20). If we don't bother to know and do the mission God has given us, the world will impose its values on us. We may end up with mission statements like these:

"My mission in life is to be rich and famous."

"My mission in life is to do everything that will give me pleasure."

"My mission in life is to get whatever is best for me at any cost."

Imagine actually putting mission statements like those on paper. Yet each of us ultimately chooses to do the work of the world or the work of God. Asking God to help us clarify our mission gives us an opportunity to participate in His marvelous works, which He has prepared for us beforehand (Ephesians 2:10).

A mission statement gives us hope for the future. Mission statements give us a promise of what's coming when we can't yet see the end. God works from faith, not sight. The world tells us, "See it, and then you will believe it." God says, "Believe, and then you will see the glory of God."

God gave Abraham this mission: Abraham would be the father of a great nation, his name would be great, and through him all the families of the earth would be blessed (Genesis 12:2-3). Abraham died before that promise was fulfilled, yet Hebrews 11:13 tells us that Abraham "died in faith" (NASB). Although he hadn't yet received what was promised, he believed it would happen. In Hebrews 11:12 we are reminded of what we now know to be true: "From this one man, and he as good as dead, came descendants as numerous as the stars in the sky and as countless as the sand on the seashore."

Mission statements give ordinary people hope as well. Recently I heard a ninety-four-year-old woman say that her mission in life was to raise children who would love Christ. With tear-filled eyes, this elderly woman talked about her godly daughter, who married a pastor and helped him start a powerful suburban church.

4. Which of the author's reasons for writing a personal mission statement is the most compelling to you? Why?

5. How do you think having a personal mission statement would make it easier to choose only the best opportunities?

6. Read Matthew 25:14-30. What were the master's expectations regarding the talents he entrusted to his servants?

7. How do you think writing a personal mission statement would help you be a better steward of the resources with which God has entrusted you?

D | Writing Your Mission Statement

How do you write a personal mission statement? The following are some practical suggestions to accomplish this life-changing activity.

Pray. As Christians we know that God has a purpose for us. Ask God to reveal your mission to you. Trust that God desires for you to do this (James 1:5). The Scriptures tell us that we have a God of clarity, not confusion. Our prayer reaps for us untold benefits.

Study the Scriptures. Our personal mission should be in harmony with the Word of God. In my law practice, I work in the area of mediation. When I recently worked on a task force to mediate disputes in a Christ-centered atmosphere, we spent one-third of our seven sessions studying the book of Colossians. Scripture is the best place to gain insight for a personal mission statement. I recommend starting with Paul's epistles.

8. Review your answers to questions 1 and 3 on page 62-63. Though Jesus' and Paul's missions weren't exactly the same, in many ways they were very similar. Summarize the common elements you see in their missions.

9. What biblical passages has God used deeply in your life?

10. How have these passages shaped the way you see life and the world?

The remaining questions are designed to help you view your life from a number of different perspectives before writing your personal mission statement. Before you begin to work on these questions, spend some time in prayer, asking God to clearly reveal His mission for you.

11. In what ways have you seen God use you significantly in the past? How has He worked through you?

12. What convictions and passions burn in your heart?

13. Think about some of the deepest disappointments you have experienced. What have those experiences taught you about the way God has wired you?

14. What are your primary strengths?

15. What do you consider to be your biggest weaknesses?

16. In your work experiences, at what have you excelled? With what have you struggled the most?

17. What achievements in your life have given you the greatest satisfaction?

18. Do you have an idea of what your primary spiritual gifts are? If so, list them below. If not, consider purchasing one of the many books on spiritual gifts to develop a better idea of how God has designed you to function in the body of Christ.

19. If you have been able to exercise your spiritual gifts, what have you learned about yourself in the process?

20. Ask two or three people close to you how they would describe your strengths, weaknesses, and passions. Have your friends' perceptions of you given you any new insights on how God has wired you?

21. List your main talents.

22. What verbs (action words) would you choose to describe what you love to do (for example: write, teach, inspire)? List as many as you can think of, then go back and pick two or three that best capture your sense of what you like to do.

23. How would you describe your personality? Does your personality give you any clues about what you might pursue, or definitely should *not* pursue, as a life mission?

24. Imagine your life ten years from now. What would you like to have accomplished by then? Consider this question in terms of each of the major areas of your life: your marriage, relationships, career, education, finances, and so on.

25. Go back and reread your answers to the questions in this session. Ask God to help you see clearly how He has designed you to operate.

   a. Do you have any new insights into the way God has designed you?

   b. What ideas do you find repeated in your answers to these questions? Repetition may indicate that you need to consider something more strongly.

   c. Which ideas did you find yourself most excited about as you wrote them down?

   d. Did any of the answers (or the whole process) cause something to click in your mind, causing you to think, *That's what I need to do?*

26. Now begin to write out phrases that capture the most important ideas you have been able to cull out of the answers to your questions. Pay close attention to the questions that dealt with your strengths, your talents, your passions, and others' thoughts about what makes you tick. If you are struggling to compose a suitable mission statement, simply put your notes down and come back in a day or two. Crafting a personal mission statement is a process that often takes some time. When you complete the process, write your personal mission statement below.

- My mission is . . .

Words Worth Remembering

But to what must we be committed? To Jesus Christ Himself—
to be in love not with a cause, but with the One who gives us
the cause.

—Bob Boardman, "A Call to Commitment," Issue Z

7

Abiding in Christ

We began this study by thinking about rest and the easy yoke. In this session, we're going to revisit the subject of peace and rest in the midst of our busy lives. We will also take another look at the priorities God wants us to focus upon. As you read this session's article, entitled **"At Peace in the Whirlwind" by Lorraine Pintus** (excerpted from Issue 97), underline the ideas that stand out to you. Then move on to the questions and exercises that follow.

AT PEACE IN THE WHIRLWIND

You punch the accelerator. The speedometer needle edges up. The world outside your window is a blur. Faster, faster you zip around the track, exhilarated by the speed and the whine of an engine pushed to the limit. Skillfully, you weave past other cars—watchful, alert. And suddenly tense.

Something is wrong. A red flag catches your eye. Your crew chief is signaling you to pull in for a pit stop. What will you do? Will you heed the warning, even though it means giving up your position? Or will you ignore the signal and press on?

Why do I keep going when the Holy Spirit urges, "Pull over"? Do I subconsciously resent someone else controlling my life? Am I prideful, thinking I know best? Is my need to perform stronger than my desire to obey? Do I fear disapproval from others?

I crash for many reasons, but the result is always the same. Peace vanishes. I become anxious, nervous. People and their needs annoy me. Hurtful words slip out. I can't sleep. God seems distant. The warning light of my life flashes "Out of Control."

1. The author describes several symptoms of an "out of control" life. What warning signs in your life indicate things are out of control?

D| Glued to Jesus

"Thou wilt keep him in perfect peace, whose mind is stayed on thee," we're told in Isaiah 26:3 (KJV). "Remain in me, and I will remain in you," says John 15:4.

According to these verses, to have peace I need only to stay glued to Christ! Easy, right? No. In the stress of daily living I often become unglued.

My seven-year-old daughter, Amanda, came home from vacation Bible school and proudly announced, "I asked Jesus into my heart." "But honey, you asked Jesus into your heart two years ago," I replied. She shrugged her shoulders and sighed. "I know. But He keeps escaping."

Like Amanda, I sometimes feel as though I can't keep Jesus in me. He unexpectedly slips away, taking His peace with Him. Actually, the reverse is true. I slip away from Jesus and leave His peace behind! I try to "fix [my] eyes on Jesus" (Hebrews 12:2), to "take captive every thought to make it obedient to Christ" (2 Corinthians 10:5). But my mind and heart wander. People and situations clamor for attention. Interruptions steal my time. Unexpected problems preempt my plans. Suddenly, I'm no longer "in Christ," but in chaos!

Still, it is possible to consistently be at peace in the midst of busyness. I know it is because Christ did it. Christ was most likely the busiest person who ever lived. Crowds pestered Him. Strangers grabbed His clothing. People with needs disturbed His sleep and interrupted His teaching. In one day alone, Jesus encouraged the disciples, healed the sick, taught the multitude, fed the five thousand, and helped a friend through a storm! All this, and He still found time to be alone with His Father (John 6:1-24).

How did Jesus remain at peace in the midst of such busyness?

He had help—supernatural help. The apostle John wrote about this in Scripture: "By myself I can do nothing" (John 5:30); "It is the Father, living in me, who is doing his work" (John 14:10).

Jesus lived a life of unbroken fellowship with His Father. It was His constant connectedness to God that enabled Him to have peace in the midst of turmoil. If I abide in Christ, I, too, can experience peace in the midst of chaos. But I must stay connected to my Lord, as Jesus stayed connected to His Father.

2. a. How can we stay "glued to Christ"? In John 15, Jesus answers this question by describing how His followers receive life and produce fruit. Read John 15:1-8 below. Circle the word "remain" each time Jesus uses it.

"I am the true vine and my Father is the gardener. He cuts off every branch in me that bears no fruit, while every branch that does bear fruit he prunes so that it will be even more fruitful. You are already clean because of the word I have spoken to you. Remain in me, and I will remain in you. No branch can bear fruit by itself; it must remain in the vine. Neither can you bear fruit unless you remain in me.

"I am the vine; you are the branches. If a man remains in me and I in him, he will bear much fruit; apart from me you can do nothing. If anyone does not remain in me, he is like a branch that is thrown away and withers; such branches are picked up, thrown into the fire and burned. If you remain in me and my words remain in you, ask whatever you wish, and it will be given you. This is to my Father's glory, that you bear much fruit, showing yourselves to be my disciples."

b. Look closely at each of the places Jesus uses the word "remain." From the context of these verses, what do you think it means to remain in Him?

3. What does remaining in Him require of His followers?

4. What are the benefits and results of remaining in Him?

5. What does Jesus say is the ultimate purpose of remaining in Him? How does this purpose motivate you?

6. Jesus said that one requirement of remaining in Him is that His words remain in us. What changes or adjustments could you make in your life to allow His Word to dwell in you more richly?

7. a. The word translated as "remain" in the NIV is translated differently in other versions. Let's look at John 15:4 in several other paraphrases to broaden our understanding of what Jesus is teaching in this passage.

    ■ "Abide in me, and I in you." (RSV)
    ■ "Remain united to me, and I will remain united to you." (TEV)
    ■ "Take care to live in me, and let me live in you." (TLB)
    ■ "You must go on growing in me and I will grow in you." (PH)

- "Make your home in me, as I make mine in you." (JB)
- "Dwell in me, as I in you." (NEB)
- "Stay joined to me, and I will stay joined to you." (CEV)
- "Live in me. Make your home in me just as I do in you." (MSG)

   b. Underline the different words and phrases these translations use instead of "remain."

8.   How do the different translations of this verse shed more light on what it means to remain in Jesus?

9.   Did one of these translations give you a new insight into what it means to "remain in Christ"? Explain.

Ⅾ Dependence

"I do nothing on my own" seemed to be the theme of Jesus' life (John 8:28). When a hemorrhaging woman touched Jesus' garment, hoping to be healed, power drained from Him. If power drained from Jesus each time He healed, why didn't He become empty? Dependence upon the Father allowed Him to draw from a well of limitless resources.

Jesus invites me to draw from this well so that I, too, need never feel empty or drained. But access to the well is only gained through wholehearted dependence upon Christ.

I must allow Jesus to be my all: the breath in my lungs, the thoughts in my head, the words on my lips. My spirit must proclaim, "Apart from [Christ, I] can do nothing" (John 15:5). My actions must declare, "I no longer live, but Christ lives in me" (Galatians 2:20).

How does this work? When I am weary but have a Bible study to teach, I picture the tired me resting in a chair while Christ in me teaches the study. When I want to look at a magazine but my children want me to read them a book, I order the selfish me to step aside while Christ in me reads Dr. Seuss's *Hop on Pop* for the millionth time. When I feel anger toward the driver who has just cut me off, the angry me moves over and Jesus in me offers a sympathetic you-must-have-had-a-bad-day wave. Much of my dependence upon Christ involves me getting out of the way so that the King of kings may speak and act through me.

10. As you read the following passages, list the ways these passages reveal Jesus' dependence upon His Father.

- Matthew 4:1-11

- Matthew 14:23

- Matthew 26:36-46

- Mark 1:35

- Luke 2:41-50

- Luke 6:12-16

- John 7:16

D Obedience

In John 15:9-10, Jesus challenges, "Remain in my love, . . . just as I have obeyed my Father's commands and remain in his love."

Jesus also said, "I love the Father and . . . do *exactly* what my Father has commanded me" (John 14:31, emphasis added). Sometimes this verse translates in my life as, "I love the Father and do pretty much what He commands me." I do not make it a point to disobey God, but neither do I make it a point to wholeheartedly follow the holy standard God prescribes. The Bible says, "Do not judge"; so instead I "discern." Scripture commands me to forgive as I have been forgiven; I sometimes forgive as I think the offender deserves. God warns, "Do not lie"; so I exaggerate.

John said, "The man who says, 'I know him,' but does not do what he commands is a liar, and the truth is not in him" (1 John 2:4).

I cannot abide if I will not obey. If the peace of God is absent from my life, perhaps it is because I am refusing to obey the Holy Spirit's warning to align my life with the Word of God.

11. The author describes several subtle forms of disobedience. Spend a few minutes asking God to bring to mind any areas of disobedience in your life that need to be dealt with. Then ask Him what specific steps you need to take to be obedient. If God brings something specific to mind, record it below.

Focus

Jesus said, "I know where I came from and where I am going" (John 8:14). Christ's every action was embedded in His purpose. He did not debate over whether or not to include certain activities in His schedule. Rather, the deliberateness of His every action spoke "That is why I have come" (Mark 1:38; see also Luke 5:32, 9:21-22, 12:49-51, and John 12:27).

Oswald Chambers writes in *My Utmost for His Highest* that we must begin with the end in mind. Focusing on the end simplifies the middle. When I fix my eyes on my end—to glorify Jesus in all I say and do—and I abide in Christ in the present, the days take care of themselves.

12. When we get too busy, it's easy to lose focus on the things that matter most. Read the following passages: Matthew 22:37, 28:18-20; Mark 10:42-45; Luke 9:23; and John 13:34, 14:21. What priorities does Jesus define for those who follow Him?

13. Of those commands and instructions, which do you feel you are following fairly well, and in which do you think you are struggling?

14. What factors in your life contribute to your success or difficulty in these areas?

15. Many of the passages in question 12 are familiar ones. Consider your reaction to reading these Scriptures. How did you react to the things Jesus says are truly important?

   ☐ I feel I'm well focused on biblical priorities.
   ☐ I think I'm doing okay. Some of these areas are priorities in my life, but I could be doing better in other areas.
   ☐ I'm not doing so well. My life doesn't reflect a focus on the things Jesus commands.
   ☐ I'm barely staying afloat as it is and, frankly, these commands just seem overwhelming.
   ☐ Other:

16. If you feel there's a gap between your knowledge of these commands and your current experience, take a few minutes to ask God to show you one or two specific adjustments you can make in your life right now. Ask God the following questions as you pray:

   ▪ Am I currently involved in any activities or commitments that You would have me step out of?
   ▪ Are there areas I need to be focusing on in my relationship with You or with others that I'm currently neglecting?
   ▪ Are there things in my life that consistently sap my time and energy that are not important or related to Your kingdom priorities?

Rest

In our performance-oriented society, many of us, like the Energizer® bunny, keep going . . . and going! But God commands us to rest (Exodus 16:23, 31:15). In the Old Testament, rest came through observing special occasions: weekly rest (the Sabbath); seasonal rest (feasts and holidays); and extended rest, as in the seventh Sabbath year in which the land and people rested. In the New Testament, rest comes through a relationship with Jesus.

Jesus proclaimed Himself "Lord of the Sabbath" (Luke 6:5), suggesting that His rest supersedes the rest found in the Law. Old

Testament rest involved occasional physical rest. New Testament rest is continual and spiritual. Old Testament rest occurred because of something the people did out of respect for God. New Testament rest occurs because of what God did out of love for His people. Jesus' death on the cross put to death my sin, the root cause of all restlessness.

How do I tap into this rest? Simply abide. The core of my every thought must be *I am in Christ and He is in me.* To rest, I have only to shut out the distractions of the world, draw deep within, and commune with my Lord in the quiet center of my heart where He resides. Though winds of conflict and waves of busyness assail me, I rest safely in the arms of the One who whispers, "Peace, be still."

Jesus wants me to combine the wisdom of the Old Testament physical rest with the concept of New Testament spiritual rest. He illustrated this as He instructed His weary disciples, "Come with me by yourselves to a quiet place and get some rest" (Mark 6:31). Such instruction reinforces what I know to be true but often forget: Apart from Christ, there is no rest.

---

17. Read Exodus 31:12-17. What was the punishment for those who failed to refrain from work and observe the Sabbath as the Lord commanded?

18. Why do you think God's instructions regarding the Sabbath were so strict?

19. What do we learn about God's purposes for the Sabbath in this passage?

20. Most of us know that we need to rest, yet often we do not take time for the rest we need. What factors can make it difficult for you to cease laboring and take a much-needed break?

☐ I don't believe I need as much rest as God says that I do.
☐ It's hard for me to trust God with the time it would take to rest when there are so many things that need to be done.
☐ I'm afraid if I slow down, I'll see issues in my life I really don't want to deal with.
☐ When I relax I feel like I should be doing something.
☐ I would have to say no to people and/or activities to which I'm currently committed.
☐ Other:

Ⓓ Prayer

Jesus prayed unceasingly. Certain prayers expressed praise; others acknowledged His ongoing fellowship with the Father. One prayer expressed agony.

In His plea for the Father to remove the cross, Jesus sweat drops of blood (Luke 22:44). He did not want to do what God was asking Him to do! Ultimately Jesus surrendered His desires to the Father's will. The cross remained, but in His mercy, God sent an angel to strengthen Jesus for what lay ahead.

Recently I agonized over something God was asking me to do. I pleaded with Him to remove the situation from my schedule, but His response was no, that He would use this to accomplish His purposes in me and in others. In His mercy, God sent two "angels," Sandy and Linda, to encourage me. Through the prayers of these friends, my burden lifted. My schedule had not changed, but now I had the peace to deal with what lay ahead.

Live One Day at a Time

Jesus said, "Do not worry about tomorrow, for tomorrow will worry about itself" (Matthew 6:34).

Panic over my schedule almost always comes from looking too far ahead in my Day-Timer®. Activities swell to tsunami size, and a giant wave of anxiety crashes down upon me.

Scripture warns us not to borrow trouble from tomorrow. God instructed the Israelites concerning the gathering of manna: "The people are to go out each day and gather enough for that day" (Exodus 16:4). Some people disobeyed and gathered the next day's manna. The extra portion spoiled and became a breeding ground for maggots.

In Luke 11:3 Jesus tells the disciples to pray, "Give us each day our daily bread." Charles Spurgeon comments on this thought in his daily devotional: "He only permits us to pray for *daily* bread and only promises that as our *day* is our strength shall be" (emphasis added).

Are you at peace in your busyness? If not, Jesus invites you: "Come to me . . . and I will give you rest" (Matthew 11:28); "Remain in me, and I will remain in you" (John 15:4). Peace in the midst of the whirlwind is that easy . . . and that difficult.

---

21. What three things are you most anxious about today? Write them below. Then, spend some time in prayer about each of these issues. Because God has promised to provide for our needs daily, consider praying, "Father, how do I need to trust You with this issue today?"

Words Worth Remembering

How do we endure? How do we gain the capacity to persevere? It isn't through our strength. It isn't because of our commitment. It isn't because we have memorized so many verses. It is because He has said, "I will never desert you, nor will I ever forsake you."

—George Sanchez, from "How to Succeed God's Way," Issue 17

8

Retreat and Reflect

This final session is designed to help you reflect more deeply on the issues you've considered in the last three sessions. One of the best ways to cement these ideas in your life is to spend a longer period of time with God than you ordinarily do. This practice is called a personal retreat.

In the first half of this session, you'll read two short articles describing what a personal retreat is, why it's important, and how to take one. These articles are entitled "**Personal Retreat: A Special Date with God,**" **by Jean Fleming** (excerpted from Issue 60), and "**Planning a Personal Retreat,**" **by Roger Fleming** (excerpted from Issue 60). The second half of this session is composed of questions and exercises to help you apply the ideas found in sessions five through seven.

D PERSONAL RETREAT: A SPECIAL DATE WITH GOD

When I worked in Washington, D.C., I often ate my bag lunch as I walked to my favorite art gallery. Then, in silence, I focused my attention on one painting, because I knew that I couldn't gallop through an art gallery and expect to appreciate it or understand what I was looking at. Works of art, literature, music, and even the glories of creation seldom yield themselves to the casual observer. Unless we purposely slow our pace and narrow our focus, we will miss the marrow of life.

This is especially true of our relationship with God. If our experience of God is bare boned (perhaps structurally sound but lacking marrow), we will drudge along, trying to obey, convinced that living the Christian life is a heavy but necessary burden. But when we take time to gaze at God, our experience is transformed.

David understood this truth. He said, "One thing I ask of the LORD, this is what I seek: that I may dwell in the house of the LORD all the days of my life, to gaze upon the beauty of the LORD and to seek him in his temple" (Psalm 27:4).

David narrowed the lens to sharpen his focus. He sought one thing: to gaze upon the beauty of the Lord. As I read the psalms, it is evident to me that David knew what it was to gaze unhurriedly at God. And the result, David said, was that his soul was satisfied (Psalm 63:5, KJV).

Taking time to focus on God and our relationship with Him is called personal retreat. The dictionary defines retreat this way: "to draw back, withdraw to a safe or private place; a period of retirement or seclusion, especially one devoted to religious contemplation away from the pressures of ordinary life."

A weekly, monthly, or quarterly date with my husband, as enjoyable as that is, is meaningful because we talk and laugh and kiss every day. The date enriches what we build day by day. Personal retreat is time with God beyond daily quiet time. It isn't meant to replace our daily meeting with the Lord, but to enhance it. Retreat, then, is a special date with God.

Why We Need Personal Retreat

Some people tell me they feel uncomfortable with the idea of personal retreat. After all, the needs around us are so great, the opportunities for service so compelling. How do we reconcile taking time away from the heat of battle when so much needs to be done?

It is precisely *because* the needs are so great and life is so short that I take personal retreats. Retreat is the way to advance. I know this is true because of the way Jesus lived.

Life for Jesus was short and busy, too. He lived on earth fully aware that the clock was ticking away. Jesus had only three-and-a-half years for public ministry, but this didn't keep Him from taking personal retreats.

Jesus modeled and taught regular withdrawal into God's presence. The gospel of Mark, the most action-packed account of the life of Jesus, shows Him continually pulling back from opportunities to minister so that He could pray and listen to His Father. His life illustrates the perfect life: one of retreat followed by intense involvement in the world.

Jesus summed it up when He said, "He will come in and go out, and find pasture" (John 10:9). Jesus gives two clarion calls: *go* and *come*. He sends us to a needy world in His name, and He calls us to draw near that He might reveal Himself to us and through us.

In Hebrews, believers are commanded to enter into the rest prepared for them. Rest signifies a state of spiritual health and well-being, not an escape into nothingness. Retreat is taking time to break the intensity of activity, to slow down, to regroup. Christian retreat is meeting with the living, personal God. It is a time to learn about God and to delight in that revelation, which is the heart of worship.

Benefits of Personal Retreat

Retreat times are "re-times"—times of refreshment, replenishing, and reflection.

Retreat rekindles our spiritual fervor for God. Scripture admonishes us, "Never be lacking in zeal, but keep your spiritual fervor" (Romans 12:11). Time set aside to seek the Lord heightens our love for Him, and He promises to reveal Himself to the ardent seeker (Jeremiah 29:13). Seeking is for our sakes. It prepares us to receive His revelation and provides uninterrupted time to respond in joy and worship to this revelation.

Personal retreat renews a steadfast spirit in us (Psalm 51:10) and restores the joy of our salvation (Psalm 51:12). It also refocuses our vision and refines our perceptions by reshaping our thinking according to God's Word (Romans 12:2). It allows us to see our tendency to drift so that we can make course corrections.

Taking the Time for Personal Retreat

Personal retreat squeezed into busy times requires commitment and savvy. How ironic that when we need a personal retreat the most, it is the most difficult to get. The pressure of a new job, or a move, or a house full of young children, or caring for the ill shrinks our time as well as our personal resources. But with creativity and commitment we can often carve out the needed respite.

Personal retreats can be measured in days or minutes. Consider setting aside a lunch hour once a week, or block out time on the weekend. Perhaps a spouse or friend can cover for you to allow a secluded Saturday morning away. Mothers of young children can trade child care for an uninterrupted date with the Lord.

When the leap from rushing to get the children delivered to a friend's house to the tranquillity of sitting with an open Bible seems too great a chasm for us, we can bridge the gap by a little bit of planning. I lay out a loose plan for my retreat the night before and decide what materials I'll take with me. A time-proven book, one that warms my heart and primes my spirit, helps me transition from bustle to stillness. I read only the amount necessary to move me from my hectic temporal thoughts to the place of quiet fellowship with Christ. Then I open my Bible and notebook. However you define it, wherever you take it, and whatever time you allot, I'm convinced of one thing: personal retreat is not luxury or indolence. It is a time of renewal so that we can experience flavor and power in our public lives. It is also an active choice we make to know God better. Just *wanting* to know Him is not enough.

1. What barriers in your life would you have to overcome to take a regular spiritual retreat?

   ☐ Time
   ☐ Money
   ☐ Spouse/family members not understanding the need
   ☐ Child care/baby-sitting
   ☐ A place to go
   ☐ Other:

2. Spend some time brainstorming, then use the chart below to record your ideas of how to overcome any obstacles in your life to taking a personal spiritual retreat.

Obstacle	Action Plan

Ⓓ PLANNING A PERSONAL RETREAT

Once you've made the decision to schedule a personal retreat, you'll need to determine what you want it to accomplish. Do you want to know God better? Do you need perspective on a particular problem? Is it time to evaluate different areas of your life and then do some strategic planning? Maybe you just want some refreshment for your soul.

After you know your goal, decide how much time you will need, when you will take the time, and where you will go. Have plan B ready in case an emergency comes up so that you don't postpone your retreat indefinitely. Next, decide on a Bible passage and collect other reading material to complement the theme. Take along a notebook or diary. Finally, consider sharing the results of your personal retreat with someone who will hold you accountable for any decisions that result from your time.

Here is a sample plan for spending time with God.

- Purpose: To know God better
- Time: Saturday 9-11 A.M.
- Place: Monument Park (library if raining)
- Plan: First, read introduction to *Knowing God* by J. I. Packer. Then, pray and meditate verse by verse through Psalm 103. Finally, make notes of thoughts about who God is and how these ideas apply to my current situation.

---

3. Create a plan for your spiritual retreat. To increase the likelihood of following through on your plan, get your calendar out right now and schedule your personal retreat below.

    - Purpose

    - Time

    - Place

    - Plan

The remainder of the questions in this session review sessions five through seven and would be excellent material for your spiritual retreat.

Session Five: Discerning God's Voice as We Make Decisions
4. In John 10:4, Jesus promised that His followers would recognize His voice. As a result of this study, how have you grown in your ability to discern God's voice in prayer?

5. a. In session five, question 20, on page 60, you identified several things that may keep you from hearing God's voice. What adjustments have you made since then that have enabled you to hear God's voice more clearly? (For example: *I've realized that constant noise in my life makes it difficult for me to sit in silence. Because of that, learning to listen to God has been hard for me. One adjustment I've made is to turn the radio off on the way to work in the morning. I'm slowly getting used to what silence is like.*)

b. If you haven't made any changes yet, choose one thing that tends to block your ability to hear God, and think about what changes would help eliminate the static.

6. a. Read the following passages, and write down your reflections for each.

   ▪ Matthew 7:7-8

   ▪ Hebrews 11:6

   ▪ James 1:5-8

b. What do these passages promise about God's willingness to answer our prayers for guidance and wisdom?

7. What role does faith play as we seek God?

8. How do you think these passages about God's guidance complement the ones we looked at in session five?

9. Which commitments in your life are causing you stress?

10. a. To get God's perspective on these things, spend a some time in attentive, listening prayer. This gives God an opportunity to respond to you in areas of need in your life. Consider asking Him some or all of the following questions, then waiting and listening for His response.

   - Lord, what are the factors causing stress in this situation?
   - Do I need to make changes in this area?
   - What do You want me to do?

   b. In the space below, record any impressions you have as you pray and listen.

Session Six: Writing a Personal Mission Statement

11. If you haven't completed your personal mission statement, spend some more time thinking about it, and work to finish it. In the space below, write your personal mission statement again.

   ▪ My mission is . . .

12. This week, share your mission statement with two or three friends who know you well. Ask them whether or not they think it fits you well. While we don't want to define a personal mission statement by taking a poll, other people's perspectives can help us in the process of defining our mission in life. Record your friends' responses below. If they think your mission doesn't fit you in some glaring way, spend some time praying about it and asking God if He's leading differently through their counsel.

13. Spend ten minutes brainstorming different ways you can begin to focus on accomplishing your personal mission.

14. With your mission statement and your brainstorming ideas in mind, what goals can you set for the next year to help you focus on what God has called you to do?

15.   What changes will you need to make in your schedule to accomplish these goals?

16.   Look at your list of current commitments again and consider these questions:

- Which commitments are closely related to your mission?
- Which of them don't have much to do with your mission statement?
- From this perspective, what changes might you need to make in your current schedule?

17.   After you have spent some time thinking through the questions about your personal mission, spend a few minutes submitting your ideas, plans, and goals to God. Ask Him to guide your life. Ask Him to speak clearly to you if any of your ideas are out of line with His purposes for your life.

Session Seven: Abiding in Christ

18. a. In session seven, you spent quite a bit of time thinking about what it means to remain, or abide, in Christ. To help describe what remaining in Him looks like, Jesus used the image of a vine and its branches (John 15:1-8). Think of another image that captures the essence of abiding in Christ. In the space on the next page, either draw a picture that illustrates remaining in Him, or tape in a picture or image from a magazine (or any

other source) that captures the essence of abiding for you. Consider placing this picture somewhere you will see it regularly to remind you of the importance of abiding in Jesus.

b. After you've drawn or taped in your picture, finish this sentence: This picture illustrates abiding in Christ for me because . . .

19. a. Now draw or find a picture of what life looks like when you do not remain in Him.

b. Spend a few minutes looking at each picture. Ask God to help you remember each image when you're struggling to remain in Him in the future.

Words Worth Remembering

The basic premise of a silent, directed retreat is twofold: First, that God gives Himself to you completely only in silence and solitude. And second, that God (to use Isaiah's imagery) has lured you into the wilderness to tell you something. He has called you there by name to speak to your heart.

—Brennan, "Living as God's Beloved," Issue 108

After you've beaten busyness, keep growing through, these studies by award-winning DISCIPLESHIP JOURNAL.

Following God in Tough Times

Even when we feel imprisoned by life's difficult circumstances, God gives us freedom to choose how we'll respond. Learn how to accept and gain perspective of tough times as you move from survival to service.

Following God in Tough Times
(Jan Johnson) $6

Growing Deeper with God

Interact with God on a personal level as you uncover the Father's heart through articles, questions, quotes, Scripture, and related exercises.

Growing Deeper with God
(Susan Nikaido) $6

Becoming More Like Jesus

Becoming like Jesus is a process, not just learning a list of rules. Based on excerpts from top *Discipleship Journal* articles, this study will help you develop His character in you as you evaluate your life, understand Jesus' teachings on character, and live them out.

Becoming More Like Jesus
(Michael M. Smith) $6

Discipleship Journal's 101 Best Small-Group Ideas

Pulled from fifteen years of the best *Discipleship Journal* articles, these fun and practical ideas will help your group grow in areas like outreach, serving, prayer, Bible study, and more!

Discipleship Journal's 101 Best Small-Group Ideas $11

Get your copies today at your local bookstore,
through our website, or by calling (800) 366-7788.
(Ask for offer **#2338** or a FREE catalog of NavPress products.)

NAVPRESS

BRINGING TRUTH TO LIFE
w w w . n a v p r e s s . c o m

Prices subject to change.